"THE WORLD'S EASIES[T]

— TO —

Buying Your First House

LARRY BURKETT

WITH KEVIN MILLER
ILLUSTRATED BY KEN SAVE

NORTHFIELD PUBLISHING

CHICAGO

Larry Burkett's Money Matters for Kids
Producer: *Allen Burkett*

For Lightwave Publishing
Managing Editor: *Rick Osborne*
Text Director: *Ed Strauss*
Desktop Publisher: *Andrew Jaster*

ISBN: 1-881273-44-X

1 3 5 7 9 10 8 6 4 2

Printed in the United States of America

Table of Contents

How to Use This Book

Shortly after leaving home, many young adults embark on a learning curve so drastic that it resembles a roller-coaster ride. Things they never did before—such as holding down a full-time job, paying bills, saving money, renting an apartment, using a credit card—suddenly become sink-or-swim survival skills. Most people fail to learn these basics while still at home and are woefully unprepared for life in the real world when they move out on their own.

The first four books in this series—*Getting Your First Credit Card, Buying Your First Car, Renting Your First Apartment,* and *Making Your First College Decision*—were written to teach you the basic life skills you need to survive in today's jungle. In the next four books, *Your First Full-Time Job, Your First Savings Plan, Planning Your First Investment,* and *Creating Your First Financial Plan,* we walked you step-by-step through getting and keeping a job, saving money, investing money, and getting and keeping control of your money.

In these four new books, *Personal Budgeting, Buying Your First House, Money and Marriage,* and *Buying Insurance,* we teach you how to pay your bills and have money left over, walk through the maze of house buying, get married without going in debt, and buy the insurance you need.

These books contain a wealth of commonsense tips. They also give sound advice from a godly, biblical perspective. It is our prayer that the books in this series will save you from having to learn these things in the "school of hard knocks."

To get the most out of these books, you should photocopy and complete the checklists and forms we've included. We provided them to help you take on these new tasks step-by-step and to make these books as practical as possible.

Each book contains a glossary to explain commonly used terms. If at any point while reading you need a clear definition of a certain word or term, you can look it up. Each book also contains a helpful index that allows you to find pages where a key word or subject is mentioned in the book.

CHAPTER I

Are You Ready to Own a Home?

"I have just one question: would the monthly mortgage payments be less than what we're presently paying in rent?"

"Well, what are you paying?"

"We're staying in my parents' work shed. Rent is free."

Are You Ready to Own a Home?

The American Dream

At one time or another, nearly everyone in North America dreams of owning their own home. Whatever your housing dreams, you probably also realize that purchasing a home can be a costly and intimidating experience. The process is constantly changing, and potential pitfalls seem to lurk around every corner. However, with a little good advice and some careful planning, your dreams of owning your own home can come true. This book will help you make it happen by showing you how to create a solid home-buying plan. This plan includes the following steps:

1) Determining your housing wants and needs
2) Assessing your financial situation
3) Finding the perfect home for you
4) Putting the financial details in place
5) Making an offer
6) Closing the deal

Owning vs. Renting

Whether to buy usually depends on how much money you have to spend. Renting is often cheaper than owning, but this isn't always the case. Plus, there are advantages and disadvantages to both situations, as the following shows.

Pros and Cons of Owning vs. Renting

Owning Pros: Property builds equity over time; sense of community, security, stability; free to change décor and landscaping; larger space (usually)

Owning Cons: Possibility of foreclosure and loss of equity; Less mobility than renting; responsible for maintenance and upkeep; tax breaks on housing costs; responsibility for property taxes; larger initial investment; more variable costs

Renting Pros: Little or no responsibility for maintenance; lower housing costs (usually); easier to move; smaller "up-front" costs; more fixed costs

Renting Cons: Maintenance done on landlord's schedule; no equity is built up; possibility of eviction; no control over rent increases; no tax breaks on housing costs; limited ability to alter or personalize living; smaller space (usually)

It's obvious that neither situation is perfect. But if you're at all concerned about developing long-term financial stability for you and your family, then buying a home is definitely the way to go. (For an even more detailed comparison of the costs of renting versus owning, go to www.ginniemae.gov. There you'll find an on-line calculator that allows you to compare the financial advantages of owning versus renting a home.)

Another Reason for Buying

As a general rule, homes appreciate in value by about 5 percent per year. (This figure will vary from region to region and year to year.) Five percent may not seem like a lot at first. You could make that much putting your money into a treasury bill or a good mutual fund. But wait, there's more.

If you bought a house for $200,000, chances are you wouldn't be able to pay it all in cash. Instead, you put down, say, 20 percent ($40,000) and pay the rest with a mortgage. At an appreciation rate of 5 percent annually, a $200,000 home will increase in value by $10,000 during the first year you own it. That means you earned $10,000 on an initial investment of $40,000. That's 25 percent! Sound better now?

Don't forget that you're also making mortgage payments and paying property taxes (as well as maintenance and other costs). However, the interest on your mortgage as well as your property taxes are tax deductible. That means you can use them to reduce your gross annual income, thus reducing the total amount of tax you pay each year.

How to Know If You're Ready

Unless you're Bill Gates or a prince from the Saudi royal family, buying a home will be the single largest and most complicated purchase you ever make. Therefore, you should put more thought and planning into this transaction than any other. Owning a home requires a large commitment of time and money. So it's important to know what you're getting into before you take the plunge. The following questions will help you determine if you're even in the ballpark.

- Do you have a steady, reliable job or other source of income?
- Have you held your present job (or a similar position in your field) for the past three years?
- Do you plan to live in the area for five years or more?
- Do you have a good record of paying your bills on time?
- Do you have few outstanding long-term debts, such as car payments?
- Have you built up a credit rating through smaller loans and credit cards?
- Do you have money for a down payment? (This is usually between 5 to 20 percent of the purchase price. Zero percent financial plans are available but not recommended.)
- Will you be able to pay a mortgage every month plus additional costs related to your new home, such as maintenance, utilities, and taxes? (Anticipate at least a 20 to 50 percent increase over what you're paying for housing right now.)

If you answered yes to most or all of these questions, you're probably in a position to begin thinking seriously about buying a home. *Alrighty now!* It's time to turn the page and start getting your financial house in order.

CHAPTER 2

How Much Can You Afford?

How Much Can You Afford?

The first step you need to take before buying a home is to get a clear picture of your financial situation. This will help you estimate the size of mortgage you'll be able to carry so you won't waste your time looking at homes that are light-years beyond your means.

Budgeting Your Way to Home Ownership

The only sure way to determine how much you can afford to spend on housing is to prepare a budget and stick to it. If you're already living on a budget, pat yourself on the back. However, if your idea of budgeting is withdrawing money from the bank machine until it seizes your client card, perhaps you should read on.

A budget is merely a plan for how you use your money. It shows you how much you're spending on housing, clothing, food, entertainment, and so forth. Once you know where every dollar is going, you're in a much better position to see how much cash can be funneled away from money-gobbling activities—such as that extra cappuccino on the way home from work—and into your housing fund.

As a first step, make a couple of photocopies of the *Monthly Income & Expenses* chart on the next page, then fill in a copy to find out where your money is going right now.

For some people, filling out this form may be like a visit to the dentist. "Am I really in *that* bad of shape?" For others, it's a real eye-opener. "Who knew I was spending so much on entertainment!" Whatever the case, you'll probably agree that knowing where your money is going is a lot better than not knowing.

Monthly Income & Expenses

Annual Income _____
Monthly Income _____

LESS
1. Charitable Giving _____
2. Tax _____

NET SPENDABLE INCOME _____

3. Housing (30%) _____
    Mortgage (Rent) _____
    Insurance _____
    Taxes _____
    Electricity _____
    Gas _____
    Water _____
    Sanitation _____
    Telephone _____
    Maintenance _____
    Other _____

4. Food (17%) _____

5. Auto(s) (15%) _____
    Payments _____
    Gas & Oil _____
    Insurance _____
    License _____
    Taxes _____
    Maint/Repair/
      Replacement _____

6. Insurance (5%) _____
    Life _____
    Medical _____
    Other _____

7. Debts (5%) _____
    Credit Cards _____
    Loans & Notes _____
    Other _____

8. Enter. / Recreation (7%) _____
    Eating Out _____
    Trips _____
    Baby-sitters _____
    Activities _____
    Vacation _____
    Other _____

9. Clothing (5%) _____

10. Savings (5%) _____

11. Medical Expenses (5%) _____
    Doctor _____
    Dental _____
    Drugs _____
    Other _____

12. Miscellaneous (6%) _____
    Toiletry, Cosmetics _____
    Beauty, Barber _____
    Laundry, Cleaning _____
    Allowances, Lunches _____
    Subscriptions, Gifts _____
      (Incl. Christmas)
    Special Education _____
    Cash _____
    Other _____

TOTAL EXPENSES _____

Net Spendable Income _____

Difference _____

Your Net Spendable Income (NSI)

The percentages beside each expense category show you the ideal amount of your Net Spendable Income (NSI)—the income available after taxes and charitable giving are deducted—that should go into each of these areas. If you came in on the low side of these amounts and wound up with a surplus, you are definitely doing something right. Now you can apply some (or all) of this surplus to your Housing fund. However, if you blew these recommended percentages sky-high and came up with a deficit, it's time to think how you can get a leash on your spending patterns.

As you can see, generally no more than 30 percent of your NSI should be spent on housing. This includes mortgage payments or rent, property taxes, utilities, repairs and mainte-nance, and telephone. If you've already hit that ceiling with the amount of rent you're paying, you should probably put off your dreams of home ownership for now, because owning a home is a virtual guarantee that these costs will go up. However, if you still have room left in your budget, roll up your sleeves and take a closer look at your financial situation.

Calculating Your TDS

To calculate the size of mortgage you qualify for, banks use something called a Total Debt Service Ratio (TDS). This is calcu-lated as the percentage of your gross annual or monthly income required to cover housing costs *and all other debts*. This includes credit cards, car loans, and student loans. From the bank's perspective, this amount cannot exceed 40 percent of your gross annual or monthly income. However, we recom-mend that it not exceed 40 percent of your *net spendable income*. Therefore, if 10 percent of your NSI is going towards debts and 30 percent is going towards housing, we recommend reducing your debt load before making an appointment with the bank. For more on how to cut costs and live on a budget, see Larry Burkett's *Financial Planning Workbook*, as well as *Your Finances in Changing Times*.

Mortgage Carrying Capacity

Now that you've budgeted the amount of money you have available for housing each month, it's time to figure out the maximum mortgage you will be able to carry with that amount. This will determine the price range of homes you will be able to afford. There are two ways to do this.

1) Go On-Line:

If you're still not sure how serious you are about buying a home and you only want a rough estimate of the mortgage you'll be able to obtain, the best thing to do is use one of the many mortgage calculators on the Internet, such as the one at Ginnie Mae (www.ginniemae.gov/ypth/2_prequal/intro_questions.htm), to figure this out. With this calculator, all you do is enter your gross income and monthly debt information, and it will calculate how much money a bank will likely lend you. However, please note that this calculator gives a rough estimate only. It does not take into account your credit rating, employment situation, and other factors that lenders consider during the loan application process. Another type of mortgage calculator, such as the one at the Home Buyer's Information Center (www.ourfamilyplace.com/homebuyer/mortcalc.html), allows you to change a number of variables in regard to your mortgage so you can get an idea of what you can afford. Adjustable variables include the amortization period of the mortgage, the interest rate, the amount of money borrowed, as well as your annual insurance and tax payments. Once all of this information is entered, the calculator figures out what your total monthly payments will be. You can play around with these figures until you get a monthly payment that falls within your budget. But don't forget: this calculator does not take into account extra home ownership costs such as maintenance fees or any renovations you may want to make to the home. These will come out of your monthly housing budget in addition to your mortgage payments. For a host of other excellent mortgage and housing related calculators, check out http://www.realestateabc.com/calculator/.

2) Apply for a Preapproved Mortgage:

On-line calculators will help you get a general idea of the mortgage you can afford. But if you want to know exactly how large a mortgage you are able to get, the best thing to do is make an appointment with your lender and apply for a pre-approved mortgage. A *preapproved mortgage* allows you to be approved for a housing loan even before you start looking for a home. This is a great idea, because it will let you know exactly what price range to look in. In addition, when it comes to negotiating with sellers, they'll take you more seriously because they know you have the cash on hand. A pre-approved mortgage also protects you from rising interest rates within the time period of the prearranged mortgage (usually sixty to ninety days).

So What's Next?

Now that you know how much money you have available for housing payments each month plus the approximate amount of money the bank is willing to loan you, it's time to figure out your housing wants and needs so you can start pounding the pavement in search of that dream abode. Let's go!

CHAPTER 3

How Much House Do You Need?

"Guess which one's my favorite."

How Much House Do You Need?

Your Wish List

A good thing to do before you begin looking for a home is to come up with a wish list of characteristics that describe your ideal home. This will help you zero in on what you're looking for when you start shopping. The best way to come up with a wish list is to ask yourself some serious questions.

1) **Location:** Do you want to live in the city, the suburbs, or the country? Think about where you work, where your children go to school, where you go to church, where you shop, where you go for recreation, and where your friends and family live. You will likely want your home located close to most of these things.

2) **Lot:** How much space do you need? Are you into landscaping and gardening or would you rather not get your hands dirty? Do you want a level lot or is a sloped lot OK? Would it bother you if the lot were irregularly shaped? How close do you want to be to your neighbors?

3) **Size:** How many bedrooms do you want? How many bathrooms? Do you want a garage? If so, one car or two? How about a garden or green space? Do you want a basement? An attic? How large should your kitchen be? How about your living room?

4) **Amenities:** Do you want a workshop? What kitchen appliances do you want? Do you want a swimming pool? How about a hot tub? Do you want a deck or a patio? A fireplace? What type of heating system do you want? Do you want air conditioning? Skylights?

5) **Condition:** Do you want a new home or a used one? Do you want to be able to just move in or would you rather spend some time remodeling or personalizing the home first? Are you in for a complete renovation job?

Wish List

Location
1. _____
2. _____
3. _____
4. _____
Lot
5. _____
6. _____
7. _____
8. _____
Size
9. _____
10. _____
11. _____
12. _____
Amenities
13. _____
14. _____
15. _____
16. _____
Condition
17. _____
18. _____
19. _____
20. _____

Note: If your wish list exceeds four items per category, either photocopy another list or write the extra items out on a blank sheet of paper. Once you're done filling out your wish list, write a description of your dream home in one or two sentences. This will help you to envision what you're looking for.

You should also take into account factors in your present and future lifestyle that will affect your housing needs. For example, if you don't have children now, do you anticipate having any in the next five years? If so, how many extra bedrooms will you need? Do you entertain often or have people come stay with you? Then you'll need a place with a large living room, dining room, and a guest bedroom.

After working through these questions, photocopy the wish list and use it to record your housing wants. As you're filling out your list, write down your wants in order of priority. For example, if you simply *must* have four bedrooms, put that at the top. However, make sure to note things that you would be willing to trade off for others. For example, you might be willing to live fifteen minutes farther from work if it means having four bedrooms instead of three. And remember: this is a wish list, so have fun with it. For now—only for now—don't worry about how realistic or expensive these items will be. The point of this exercise is for you to envision your ultimate housing situation.

Time for a Reality Check

Now it's time to step back into the cold, hard world of reality and convert your wish list into a reality check. While a wish list includes everything you want in a home, a reality check lays out the minimum you will *need* to be comfortable. Photocopy another wish list form; only this time write down your *needs* instead of your *wants*.

Once you've completed your reality check, try to put all of your needs into one or two sentences just as you did for your wish list. This will give you an idea of the simple, bare necessities you're looking for in a home.

CHAPTER 4

Different Types of Homes

"You're seriously thinking of buying this . . . place?"

"Ahh, you see only with your eyes, my friend! This house can be enlarged and renovated, but look around you. It's this kind of neighborhood we really want to live in."

Different Types of Homes

When most people think of buying a home, the first thing they picture is a house. Ah, but there are several other options available. The following is a brief description of each, including their advantages and disadvantages. You may already have a good idea of what type of housing you're looking for, but read this list in case it includes some options you haven't considered and might want to.

Single-Family Detached: This is a freestanding home on its own lot that is occupied by one family. This is the typical "dream home."

Advantages: Single-family detached homes usually offer more space than the other options. They also have the highest resale value, offer more privacy, and allow you to modify or increase your living space as desired.

Disadvantages: You are responsible for all maintenance and repair costs, including landscaping. Detached houses are also the most expensive option, and they usually lack certain amenities, such as pools and playgrounds, offered by some other housing options.

Semidetached: This is a single family home that is joined to another home by a common wall.

Advantages: These are usually cheaper than detached homes. They also offer more room and a higher resale value than condominiums, town houses, or apartments.

Disadvantages: You will be much closer to your neighbors than in a detached home. These homes also don't have as high a resale value as detached homes and usually have smaller yards.

Duplex/Triplex/Fourplex: A housing arrangement where a building is divided into two, three, or four units. These units can either be side by side or located one on top of the other.

Advantages: They are usually about half the price of detached homes. They also have smaller yards, so less upkeep and maintenance is needed.

Disadvantages: They offer even less space than semidetached homes. You will also lose privacy, because you will be living even closer to your neighbors. They also have a lower resale value (duplexes, that is, not your neighbors) than detached homes, and you are not able to add on to or alter your living space as much as in a single-family home.

Row or Town House: One of several single-family homes joined by common walls.

Advantages: Less exterior maintenance and repairs. You also may have a higher sense of security being in such close proximity to your neighbors. Town house communities may also offer certain amenities, such as a pool or playground, not available with other options.

Disadvantages: You usually have to pay homeowner's association fees for upkeep and maintenance. You also have less privacy compared to single-family homes. In addition, town house complexes usually have oodles of regulations restricting the amount and types of changes you can make to the interior and exterior of your home. Plus, you may start to feel as if you're living in a fishbowl where everyone can see your every move.

Condominium: A condominium is an apartment that you own. That means you own everything inside your apartment only. However, you are also a joint owner of the exterior of the condominium complex along with the rest of the condominium owners.

Advantages: You are responsible for little, if any, exterior maintenance or repairs. Many condominiums also offer a number of amenities, such as pools and workout rooms (hey, that's pretty good) and are located close to employment and shopping centers. In addition, condominiums are usually cheaper than most other forms of housing. (Cheaper is also good.)

Disadvantages: You don't do maintenance, but you do pay a condominium association fee. You also give up a lot more of your privacy, because you're surrounded by your neighbors. Condominiums also have a reputation for being difficult to sell, and many complexes have been plagued by poor construction, and the condo owners usually have to foot the bill for extensive repairs due to leaks and flooding. Make sure you investigate the building *very* carefully before you buy.

Mobile or Manufactured Homes: A factory-built, single family home that is transported to your chosen location.

Advantages: The main attraction of mobile homes is their low cost compared to other types of housing. They also offer more privacy than apartments, condos, or town houses.

Disadvantages: The main disadvantage to mobile homes is finding a place to put them, other than in a trailer park, that is. If you do locate it in a trailer park, you are rarely able to buy the land your trailer sits on. So you become a tenant of sorts. You'll own your dwelling, but you'll also be paying rent for a place in the park. In addition, mobile homes rarely increase in value.

Co-op Housing: Co-op housing is similar to condominiums or town houses. However, instead of purchasing your unit, you actually buy a share of stock in the complex.

Advantages: A low up-front cost compared to owning your own home. Also, if you like the idea of a communal setting, co-op housing is a good option. Co-ops also require less maintenance than a house, and, as part of the community, you will have a say in who else is allowed in.

Disadvantages: As part owner of the complex, this means you are responsible to help pay for maintenance and repairs to the entire complex and are liable for the cooperative's debts. (These are definitely disadvantages.) Your investment also does not appreciate in value as it would if you owned your own home. Co-ops also have fairly restrictive regulations for their members. Plus, it takes a lot of time and effort to be a co-op participant. Remember: with a co-op, you're not really buying, you're joining!

Acreage or Hobby Farm: This is a home located on a lot of one acre or more situated on the outskirts of a city or town. Hobby farms also include outbuildings, such as a chicken coop, barn, and shop, in addition to the home.

Advantages: Good, clean country living away from the hustle and bustle of the city. You're free to roam across your property in your *lederhosen* yodeling at the top of your lungs or playing your bagpipes without worrying about your neighbors complaining. There's also room for a garden, a tree house, an orchard, a fishpond, a horse—you name it! There are also generally fewer zoning restrictions on acreages than there are in other types of housing situations.

Disadvantages: Acreages and hobby farms are one of the most expensive forms of housing out there. Bringing in electricity and phone lines (if it's not already there) will cost you extra. You will also need a well and a septic tank. That latter will have to be emptied regularly. Garbage disposal is also up to you, as is snow removal. And because you're probably not located anywhere close to a fire hydrant, you'll have to pay extra for your home insurance. In addition, taxes will be higher because your property is larger and you have to pay more for things like road upkeep and schools than you do in the city.

New Homes vs. Used Homes

Advantages of New

- You may be able to choose or upgrade building materials, floor plan, and features, such as siding, flooring, and cabinets.
- Your home will meet the latest safety and energy-efficiency standards.
- Everything is in brand-new condition, including the structure, fixtures, appliances, and other amenities.
- New homes generally appreciate in value faster than existing homes.
- You may find it more personally satisfying if you take an active role in the house building process.

Disadvantages of New

- Amenities such as schools or shopping may not be complete if the home is in a newly developed area.
- There may be construction noise and traffic noise for a while.
- There may be little or no landscaping or trees.
- New homes generally cost more than existing homes.
- Buying new is more complicated, because it involves finding a lot, a builder, a construction loan, and so on.

Advantages of Used

- Landscaping, fencing, and other exterior upgrades are usually complete.
- The neighborhood is usually more established.
- The home may include upgrades, such as a swimming pool, finished basement, or deck.
- Older homes generally have more character than newer homes.
- Used homes cost less than new homes.

Disadvantages of Used

- Maintenance costs will be higher than for a new home.
- You may need to seriously renovate.
- You will require a professional home inspection prior to purchasing.
- You have to use an existing floor plan rather than designing your own.
- Used homes appreciate in value more slowly than new homes.

Another thing to note here is that few first-time homebuyers can afford to order a new, custom-built home. Most people purchase new homes in a new subdivision or housing development instead. These homes are a bit cheaper because contractors are able to mass produce them by building them all according to a limited number of styles and floor plans. Customers usually get their pick of five or more styles and floor plans, all of which can be modified slightly. They also have a say in floor coverings, paint, fixtures, and other amenities. But even with these options, you'll probably have to make some compromises to keep things within your budget and within the contractor's limitations.

CHAPTER 5

Buying a Home with Resale Value

"Wow . . . now, this is my style!"

"Yeah, a lot cheaper than a brand-new house but twice the home."

Buying a Home with Resale Value

Once Upon a Time ...

You can't believe your eyes: You've been scanning the real estate papers for weeks now searching for that ideal home. But somehow it always seems just out of reach. Wrong price, wrong location, wrong number of bedrooms, you name it.

Then you spot it: a two-story home with hardwood floors, two fireplaces, and a front porch—just like you always dreamed! And, best of all, the asking price is within your range. Faster than you can say "preapproved mortgage," you're on the phone with your realtor setting up an appointment.

You finally arrive at the house, and it's even more wonderful than you imagined. It's in fabulous shape, and the lot has been carefully groomed and manicured.

There's a quaint little wrought iron bench under the oak tree, so you plunk yourself down to dream. How serene, how quiet, how positively delightful, you think. But wait. What's that sound—a dim rumbling off in the distance? The rumbling soon turns into a roar that grows to the point where it pounds every other thought out of your brain. Before you know it, a whistle sounds, and you look up to see—can it really be true?—a freight train barreling down the tracks a mere fifty feet from your backyard!

No, no, no, no, no! This can't be! It was so perfect . . .

You turn to your realtor, hoping for something, anything, to make it all better.

"It only comes through twice a day," he yells as he puts his hands over his ears and smiles.

"Oh, really?" you respond weakly. You can work around this somehow.

"The seller's really motivated," the realtor adds. "I think they're willing to negotiate on their price."

No wonder, one part of your brain says, they're living fifty feet from a rail yard!

But before that part of your brain can respond, your mouth takes over.

"I'll take it."

"What?" the realtor yells.

"I said, I'll take it!" Part of your brain can't believe what you're saying, but it's already been bound and gagged.

"Great!" the realtor says. He chuckles inside. Good thing this sucker didn't bother to check out the wiring or plumbing in this dying monster.

The above example is a little extreme, but it gives you a good idea of how emotions can override common sense when it comes to purchasing a home, causing you to buy something you'll regret big time later on. When it comes to choosing a home, there are two main questions you need to answer: 1) How am I going to buy it? and 2) How am I going to get rid of it later on? This chapter focuses on the second question.

Factors Affecting Resale Value

If you think about it, many of the same things that make the home appealing to you will also make it appealing to *others* down the road. However, if you haven't stopped to think through potential problems with the home, such as its location, structural integrity, or size, you may find yourself in a heap of trouble when it comes time to sell. (This principle *also* applies if you bought a leaking condo.)

The best way to avoid this problem is to be aware of potential pitfalls going in. Don't misunderstand: it's still very important to buy a home that meets your housing wants and needs. However, you should make sure that the home will appeal to the largest number of future home buyers as possible. Let's take a look at some of the many factors that can make or break a home's resale appeal.

Location, Location, Location

An old cliché among real estate agents is that the three most important factors about a home are: location, location, and location. Why do they say this? Simple: you can change nearly everything about your home, including the floor plan, the roof, the color—you name it. You can even tear most homes down and build a new one. But, unless you bought a mobile home, one thing you simply cannot change about your home is its *location*. And location has a huge effect on resale value.

For example, if your "dream" home is located next to railway tracks, this will limit the home's ability to appreciate in value. It will also limit the number of people who will be interested in buying your home in the future. Poor locations to watch out for include:

- Next to a garbage dump
- Next to a freeway, highway, busy street, or intersection
- In the center of loud, nightlife activity
- In a run-down or crime-ridden neighborhood
- In a community on the brink of economic collapse
- In a community with high property tax rates or utility rates
- Next to an industrial area full of noise and air pollution

In regard to town houses, duplexes, or condominiums, you'll also want to check into the type of people who are living in the complex. Is the complex geared towards adults or families? Do most of the people who live in the complex own or rent? How good has the condo association or owner of the complex been at maintaining the landscaping and exterior of the building? Has the complex had any problems with leaks or flooding? Find out as much as you can about these things up front.

The value of a location is not just influenced by negative factors. Many *positive* factors can also increase a location's perceived value. Some examples are:

- New development and expansion. Homes located in growing areas will appreciate in value much quicker than homes in older areas.
- Close proximity to schools, parks, shopping, public transportation, recreation centers, and other community resources.
- Being located on a quiet side street or lane or, alternatively, being located close to the heart of the action, such as right downtown.
- Being located on a corner lot as opposed to the middle of the street. This reduces the number of neighbors located right

next to your home. The same holds true for corner suites in condominiums or end units in town house complexes.

The Home

Although location is probably the most important factor affecting resale value, the size and condition of the home itself also plays a role. For example, three- and four-bedroom homes are the most popular among home buyers. Other appealing factors include:

- A deck or patio
- Hardwood floors
- A large, modern kitchen
- A finished basement
- Walk-in closets and en suite
- Multiple bathrooms
- Central air conditioning
- Energy-efficient windows
- Insulated garage
- A balcony
- A fireplace
- Modern cabinetry
- A large master bedroom
- Bay windows
- A den
- Central vacuum
- High efficiency furnace
- Workshop or shed

Don't Pay Too Much for Perks

If a home doesn't have many of these features, that doesn't mean it won't be appealing. They just help to sweeten the deal. However, be wary of paying too much for these extras, because you may not get your money back down the road. Just because you're willing to pay more for a view doesn't mean all of your prospective buyers will. If you're going to pay extra for these items, do it for your own enjoyment, not as an investment. On the downside, you should avoid buying a home if it has:

- Structural flaws
- A tiny kitchen
- Small windows
- Poor insulation
- A cracked foundation
- Small, cramped bedrooms
- Outdated wiring or plumbing
- No laundry facilities

The Lot

The piece of land the home sits on also plays a major role in the home's resale value. The key factor concerning the lot is its size. Some people want a small lot so they don't have a lot of maintenance or upkeep. Others want a large lot to give them some distance from their neighbors and to allow them to try their hand at landscaping or gardening. Other features you might want to look for when it comes to a lot include:

- A level, rectangular shape
- Large, mature trees and shrubs
- Room for gardens
- A swimming pool or hot tub
- Good sunlight
- Both front and backyard
- Established landscaping
- A well-maintained fence
- A greenhouse or shop

A Few More Factors to Consider

There is a "push/pull" effect at work in the world of real estate. For example, if someone builds a large home on a street where most homes are considerably smaller, that could work to either push the prices of the small homes up or to pull the price of the larger home down.

A good rule of thumb is to buy the worst house on the best street rather than the best house on the worst street. It's that old "push/pull" effect again. The houses on the nice street will help the one ugly home (yours) appreciate in value, if only in the value of the lot the home sits on. However, the houses on the ugly street will pull the value of the nice home down, because people will think the neighborhood is going to pot.

Finally, always be wary of a home that's been on the market for a long time. There's usually a good reason for that. Perhaps it has a poor location, a faulty structure, or some other major problem. It may *look* like a bargain, but a deal is only a deal if you get something you want—not to mention something others will want to buy from you later on down the road.

CHAPTER 6

Finding a Good Real Estate Agent

"Uhh . . . Dear? I think the real estate agent is here."

"Welll . . . maybe not quite yet. I have a feeling this one might be a little out of our league."

"Great! Maybe now we can finally do some serious house hunting!"

Finding a Good Real Estate Agent

Do I Really Need an Agent?

The short answer is no, you do *not* need a real estate agent when buying a home. There's nothing stopping you from grabbing the real estate pages and pounding the pavement in search of a home without professional real estate assistance. You can even negotiate a price on your own, although you'll need a lawyer to help you with the paperwork. However, the real question may not be whether you *can* buy a home on your own but whether you *want* to.

Real estate agents exist for a reason: buying real estate is a complicated process. Without professional help from someone who knows the business, you can very easily get taken for a ride. For example, do you know anything about determining the value of a home? Do you have an intimate knowledge of how much similar homes have sold for in the neighborhood over the past few years? Are you aware of new developments in the area that may affect property values, either positively or negatively?

For Sale by Owner

Another downside to going without an agent is that the only properties you have to choose from are those in the "for sale by owner" category, because they're the only ones where agents aren't already involved on the seller's end. And such properties are few and far between. If you choose to buy a listed property on your own, you'll have to negotiate with the seller's agent, and he or she will definitely not have your interests in mind.

Another good reason to go with a real estate agent is that it's free, at least for you. Real estate agents earn their living through commissions, which are paid by the *sellers* not the buyers. That means you get all the benefits of professional help with none of the costs. But be careful. Not every agent has your best interests in mind.

Three Types of Real Estate Agencies

One of the most common mistakes first-time homebuyers make is to assume that a real estate agent will automatically represent them in the buying process. Not so. The seller is paying the commission, so unless the agent tells you otherwise *in writing*, he or she is working for the seller.

But don't despair! That's only one type of agency relationship. You do have other options. Below is a description of three types of real estate agencies.

Seller Agency: This is the situation described above. Unless you're told otherwise, all real estate agents represent and owe allegiance to the seller—the person who pays their commission. Makes sense, doesn't it? If you contact an agent who has property listed in the newspaper or on the Internet, he or she will automatically be representing the seller. Seller's agents can still be very helpful to you throughout the buying process. After all, they want you to buy a home from them, and if you're not satisfied, they won't get paid. However, there are also several things they can't do for you:

- Tell you what to offer for the property. Their job is to help the seller get as much for his or her property as possible, not cut you a deal. And be careful: a seller's agent is free to tell the seller anything you share about your own financial situation that may influence how much you're willing to pay for the home.
- Tell you why the owner is selling.
- Tell you any concessions the seller is willing to give up in order to make a deal.
- Tell you which home to buy if you are deciding between two or more choices. A seller's agent works for each seller simultaneously, so if he or she is representing three homes, all of which you like, it would be unethical for him or her to recommend one home over the other. The agent cannot favor one seller over another.
- Point out defects in a home, unless they are hidden defects that may affect the value of the home. In other words, a seller's agent will never tell you anything to dissuade you from buying a property unless he or she is legally bound to do so.

35

- In addition, a seller's agent will usually not volunteer any information about comparable properties in the area to help you come up with a reasonable offer. They are not legally prohibited from doing so, but if you don't mention it, they sure won't.

Buyer Agency: With this type of agency, the real estate agent represents the interests of the buyer above all others. This arrangement has several obvious advantages over going with a seller agency. For example, a buyer's agent can:

- Give you any information he or she has been able to obtain about the seller, including their reason for selling, potential concessions, and any other helpful information about their financial situation.
- Volunteer information on what other, similar properties have sold for in the neighborhood. This is called *Comparable Market Analysis (CMA)*.
- Recommend what to offer on the property.
- Help you decide between two or more properties you're interested in, because he or she doesn't owe any loyalty to the sellers.
- Point out any defects in a home that may affect its value.

Dual Agency: This is when two agents (or possibly the same agent) working for the same broker each represent a buyer and a seller in a transaction. Both buyer and seller must agree to this arrangement prior to negotiations. This situation has many of the same advantages as going with a strictly buyer's agency agreement. However, you will likely have less confidence in your agent's ability to represent your interests above those of the seller.

What to Look for in an Agent

Now that you've considered the various real estate agent options, it's time to think about what you are looking for in a real estate agent as an individual. You're going to be spending a lot of time with this person, so you'd better make sure you can work together. You may already have your own list of things you're looking for in a real estate agent, but the agent "must have" the following:

- An understanding and concern for your needs
- A willingness to work with you until your housing needs are fulfilled
- A professional attitude and approach to the real estate business
- A familiarity with the area in which you're interested
- A familiarity with what's available within your price range
- Professional accreditations or designations
- Strong references from previous buyers

Where to Find an Agent

You should have no trouble finding a real estate agent. Every town or city has at least one, if not several, real estate offices, usually in the downtown area. Check your yellow pages for listings. Some other good sources include:

- Newspapers and real estate magazines. In particular, look for ads that offer buyer representation.
- Referrals from friends, relatives, and coworkers. Talk to them about their experiences, both good and bad. Would they use this agent again?
- The Internet. There is seemingly no end of real estate agents and agencies on the Internet. You should be able to search by region, company, or even by name. Some good starting points include:
  - The Home Buyer's Information Center (www.ourfamily place.com/homebuyer/agentfind.html)
  - HomeGain (www.homegain.com)
  - Yahoo (www.yahoo.com). Just enter "realtors," "real estate agents," or "real estate agencies" in the search window. It will bring up a page that allows you to search by region.
  - Another alternative is to enter names of well-known national real estate companies into a search engine. Each company should have a regional office near you.

Ten Questions to Ask a Prospective Agent or Broker

Once you find an agent, it's important that you interview him or her to see whether or not he or she is the person you're looking for. Keeping in mind the list of qualities you're looking for in an agent, be certain to also ask the following questions to get a feel for his/her skills and abilities. Photocopy this form and take it with you to your first interview.

1. How long have you been in the real estate business?
2. How long have you been with your present company?
3. How many home sales did you complete in the past two years?
4. What is the average price of the homes you sold during that time period?
5. How many buyers are you presently working with? How many sellers? (This will determine how much time the agent can devote to you.)
6. Do you normally work with sellers, buyers, or both? How about first-time buyers?
7. Can you give me the names and contact information for three buyers you have worked with so I can check with them as a reference?
8. What are the primary neighborhoods or communities in which you work?
9. What style of home do you most frequently sell?
10. How often will I hear from you? Are you planning any extended vacations over the next six months?

CHAPTER 7

Financing Your Purchase

"What is the matter with him?"

"We've spent the last few days looking at all the . . . complexities . . . involved with mortgages, loans, and amortization periods. I think his brain has reached the limit of its storage capabilities."

Financing Your Purchase

There are a number of ways you can buy a home: paying cash, institutional loans, government financing, and seller financing. We'll take a look at each option in turn.

Paying Cash

This is the best way to buy a home. If you can pay cash, a good idea is to buy a smaller "starter" home first. Do some improvements on it to increase its value and then, in a few years or so, sell it for a profit. Then use that money to buy a slightly larger home. Go through the same improvement process with this second home until you're able to sell it for a profit. If you keep doing this, you should eventually be able to move into your dream house . . . debt free. But you'd better not mind moving!

Mortgages

The type of loan you get for buying a home is called a *mortgage*. There are as many different mortgage options as there are financial institutions. However, most fall into three main categories:

Fixed Rate Mortgages: With this type of mortgage, you agree to a fixed term (say, fifteen or thirty years) and a fixed interest rate throughout that term. This is one of the best types of mortgages, because you know exactly what your interest rate and payments will be each month so you can see whether or not it will fit within your budget. It also allows you to lock into a low interest rate if you're worried that interest rates are going to go up. However, you pay for this security by agreeing to take on a slightly higher interest rate than other options offer.

Adjustable Rate Mortgages: With this type of mortgage, your interest rate will be adjusted up or down according to current interest rate levels. Thus, your monthly mortgage payments will fluctuate along with the interest rate. For example, you may start out by negotiating a $100,000 mortgage at 6.5 percent with monthly payments of $640. But two years later, the interest rate may double, raising your interest payments to $1280 a month. So be careful! Nevertheless, this is a good option if you can get a preliminary interest rate of at least 2 percent less than the fixed rate option. It is also a good option if you anticipate that interest rates are on their way down. (Once you think they've reached their lowest point, then it's a good idea to renegotiate your mortgage so you can lock in to a fixed rate.)

Payday Mortgages: This is either an adjustable rate or a fixed rate mortgage that allows you to make one half of your mortgage payment every two weeks or one-quarter payment every week instead of once a month. (These payments are usually due around the same time as you get paid, hence the mortgage's name.) The advantage is that you pay less interest each month because you're chipping away at your principal more frequently. Paying weekly or biweekly also allows you to make the equivalent of one extra mortgage payment each year. On a 30-year mortgage where you borrowed $100,000 initially, you'll save more than $60,000 in interest over the life of the loan and reduce the term of your mortgage by seven to nine years! So take this option if you can get it.

Assumable Mortgages: This is an existing fixed rate or variable mortgage that the buyer assumes from the seller. The interest rate and mortgage payments are usually lower than current rates. Sellers sometimes offer assumable mortgages if they're trying to unload their home in a hurry.

What's an Amortization Period?

One of the key questions you should ask is how long you want your mortgage to last: five, ten, fifteen, twenty, or even thirty years? This is called the loan's amortization period and will determine the size of monthly mortgage payments you make. The longer the amortization period, the lower your monthly payments will be. However, the lower your payments and the longer your amortization period, the more interest you pay in the long run. Just take a look at these numbers:

Making larger monthly payments will definitely reduce your pain and suffering later on. Just think what you could do with $30,000, the money you would save by choosing a 15-year mortgage instead of a 20-year mortgage!

Amortization Period Payment Comparisons

Calculations for a $100,000 mortgage at 8.5 percent, compounded semiannually.

Amortization	Payments	Total Paid	Total Interest
15 years	$976	$176,667	$76,667
20 years	$859	$206,667	$106,667
25 years	$795	$240,000	$140,000
30 years	$754	$268,000	$168,000

Other Ways to Save Money

Shop around for a good interest rate. The lower your interest rate, the less you pay in the long run. Be careful about "deceptive" marketing in this area. Many lenders advertise a low interest rate, but if you read the fine print, you find that it is only applied to the first year of the mortgage. After that, they crank it back up again.

Make a larger down payment. Most institutions require a down payment of between 5 to 20 percent. (Although "no down payment" loans are now available, we advise against them because they give you no equity in the home and increase your mortgage payments dramatically.) The lower down payment options are usually reserved for first-time buyers. However, you should remember that the more you put down up front, the smaller your loan will be and the lower your monthly mortgage payments will be. So strive to make as large a down payment as you can. This may mean you have to put off buying a home until you can save a little more, but it's definitely worth it.

Prepaying on your principal is a way of throwing some extra money at your loan each month or each year to reduce the amount of money the bank is charging you interest on. You'd be amazed at how much just a few extra dollars each month can reduce the amount of interest you pay on your mortgage. For example, by paying $25 extra each month on a fixed rate, 30-year $100,000 mortgage at 7 percent interest, you can save $18,214 in interest and shorten the term of your loan by more than three years. If you pay as much as $100 extra each month against your principal, that same mortgage will be reduced by at least ten years, saving you over $60,000 in interest!

The only caution is to make sure there isn't a prepayment penalty clause in your mortgage agreement. Lenders sometimes put these in to prevent you from reducing the amount of interest you pay them. (After all, that's how they make their money!)

Comparing Mortgages

It's a good idea to research the mortgage options offered by at least three lenders before you make your final choice. That will give you a good idea of what's available on the market. Each lender will likely have many options for you to consider. A good way to do this is on the Internet. Several web sites will do this for you for free. Here are four sites to get you started:

- **www.lendingtree.com** — This site allows you to fill out and submit a single loan application and receive up to four competing mortgage offers within two business days.

- **www.moneyextra.com** — This site will allow you to compare over 4,900 mortgage options offered by 140 lenders and then apply on-line.

- **www.quickenmortgage.com** — This site will help you explore mortgage options and apply for a home loan on-line.

- **www.realestate.com** — This is a great comprehensive real estate site that will help you find a mortgage broker or connect with other home financing professionals.

How to Apply for a Mortgage

Once you've chosen a lending institution or mortgage broker (a company that works on behalf of other financial institutions but doesn't actually provide the funding for your loan), your next step is to make an appointment to go in and fill out the loan application.

It's very important at this point to get all of your financial and personal documentation in order. A lack of documentation will result in a delay in the loan approval process, which could mean that you're missing out on that dream home. The following is a checklist of the main documents your loan officer may ask for. Before you start the loan approval process, make sure you're able to get hold of these documents immediately, if requested.

Loan Application Checklist

- W2 forms for anyone whose name will appear on the loan application.
- Tax return forms for each co-borrower for the past three years, including schedules and attachments.
- Three months of pay stubs for each co-borrower.
- Proof of any other income you have.
- Copies of the three most recent statements for every bank account, IRA, 401(k), stock account, or any other asset you or your co-borrower own.
- Addresses and account numbers for every form of credit you have, including credit cards and lines of credit.
- A list of your addresses for the past seven years.
- Copies of an old survey or title policy for the home, if available. You should be able to get this from your real estate agent or from the municipality.
- If you have previously declared bankruptcy, you will need to supply a complete copy of the bankruptcy proceedings as well as a letter explaining the circumstances of the bankruptcy.
- A copy of the sales contract.

Please note that this information will also be required even if you apply for a mortgage on-line.

Your Credit History

Prior to applying for a loan, find out if there are any black marks on your credit history. This includes things like unpaid phone bills, defaults on student loan payments, and so on. Your lending institution is going to investigate your credit history as part of the loan application process. So if there are any skeletons in the closet, it's best that you discover and deal with them, or you'll be wasting your time down at the bank.

For a free credit report, visit www.freecreditreport.com. You can also obtain a credit report for a small fee—usually between $5 to $20—from one of the three major credit reporting companies in the Unites States. You're advised to contact all three organizations just in case one of them has made a mistake.

If a mistake has been made—for example, if they say you never paid a particular bill when you actually did—you should be able to correct it by writing to the company and providing them with written proof of the error. The contact information for each company is as follows:

- Equifax: www.equifax.com or1-800-685-1111
- Trans Union: www.transunion.com or1-800-916-8800
- Experian: www.experian.com or 1-800-682-7954

Government Financing

Apart from mortgages, another way to finance your home is through a subsidized government loan. The government department responsible for this loan program is the Federal Housing Administration (FHA), which operates under the jurisdiction of the Department of Housing and Urban Development (HUD). The FHA's job is to make purchasing a home easier for people with low incomes or poor credit records.

It works is like this: Lenders don't always feel comfortable loaning money to first-time home buyers, especially if the buyers are only making a small down payment. So the FHA provides lenders with mortgage insurance to help minimize the lender's risk.

The good thing about the FHA is that you don't need a perfect credit history or a high-paying job to qualify for a loan. You also don't need as large a down payment as you do with conventional loans, in some cases as low as 3 percent of the purchase price, and your monthly payments may also be lower. However, as you know, low payments may help you now when cash is tight, but the less you pay up front, the more you pay in interest over the life of the mortgage and the more your home will cost in the long run. You're also not allowed to roll closing costs into an FHA loan. However, you may be able to include them as part of your down payment. Your lender will give you all the details you need. For more information on the FHA and HUD, visit www.hud.gov.

Seller Financing

Another way to purchase a home is for the seller to finance the home for the buyer. This is a rare situation, but it is a sweet deal if you can get it, because you will probably save a percentage or two on your interest rate, and you won't have to pay closing costs.

Conclusion

Figuring out your best financing options is almost as much work as finding a home. It's obvious that paying cash is your best option. But if this is not possible, make sure you take time to thoroughly investigate all of your financing options *before* making your choice. For more detailed insights into mortgages and other financing options, check out the websites mentioned above. The following books and additional websites will also help.

Books

Bradley, Beth, and Alan J. Perlis. *The Unofficial Guide to Buying a Home*. New York: Hungry Minds, Inc., 1999.

Glink, Ilyce R. *100 Questions Every First-Time Home Buyer Should Ask*. New York: Random House, 2000.

Tyson, Eric, and Ray Brown. *Home Buying for Dummies*. New York: Hungry Minds, Inc., 2001.

Irwin, Robert. *Tips and Traps When Buying a Home,* 2nd ed. New York: McGraw Hill, 1990.

Websites

www.crown.org — This is Crown Financial Ministries website. Here, you'll find articles, tips, and tools to help you learn about buying a home.

www.moneyextra.com — This site provides tons of information on home buying and financing.

www.ourfamilyplace.com — This is one of the best sites out there when it comes to answering questions that first-time home buyers ask. You can also use this site to find agents and apply for financing.

CHAPTER 8

Buyer Beware!

"All right . . . maybe the floor is just a bit out of level?"

Buyer Beware!

We've already addressed a number of potential dangers related to choosing a home, a real estate agent, and a financing option. But there are several *other* things you should be aware of, particularly when it comes to looking at used homes.

Always Look a Gift Horse in the Mouth

Remember the railway home? One of the most common mistakes made by first-time homebuyers is to buy with their hearts, not their heads. Want to avoid doing this? Then examine the home thoroughly before you buy it. (See Proverbs 22:3.)

Don't be afraid to snoop and ask questions. We highly recommend getting a professional home inspector to examine a home before you buy it (more on that below). But before you call in the experts, there are still plenty of things you can be on the watch for. Some of these things you can probably fix. *But!* Many of them are signs that there may be more problems with this home than meets the eye. Photocopy the checklist on page 50 and take it with you when you examine a potential home.

Hire a Professional Home Inspector

Unless you're very knowledgeable about homes and home construction, you're going to need an expert to make sure the place isn't a money-sucking black hole. Sure, getting a home inspection will cost a bit of money, but it's a small price to pay to avoid shelling out tens of thousands of dollars in repairs later on.

You can find listings for home inspectors in your yellow pages. Your realtor may also be able to supply you with some contact information. But be careful: the inspector should be an independent third party, not someone who owes allegiance to the real estate broker or the seller.

A home inspection typically takes between two to three hours. The inspector's report will cover the same areas you looked at in your own walk-through. You should go along with the inspector and be sure to ask lots of questions. He or she will be knowledgeable about things to watch for with new and used homes and will be able to point out things you couldn't see on your own.

If Your Inspector Finds Problems

It's virtually guaranteed that your home inspector will find one or several problems with the home you're looking at, especially if it's an older home. However, that doesn't mean you should scratch the home off your list.

Fixable problems include things like water damage, a dilapidated roof, poor seals around the windows, and so forth. Unfixable problems include things like a cracked foundation or a contaminated water supply. If your prospective home has an unfixable problem, of course you shouldn't buy it. However, if it has some fixable problems, you'll have to make some decisions. First of all, are the problems major or minor? Is it worth fixing them at the present asking price or should you use them to help you bargain for a lower price? If you and the seller have already agreed on a tentative price for the home, don't draw back due to a doorknob that won't turn properly or a broken windowpane. Be reasonable, but don't let yourself get walked on either.

Home Inspection Checklist

Property Address: _____

Exterior Description: _____

- *Foundation:* Are there any obvious cracks or other defects, such as signs of shifting?
- *Roof:* What is its overall condition? How old is it? How long until it will need to be replaced?
- *Evidence of leaks:* Check all ceilings and areas around windows for signs of water damage. Do this both inside and outside of the home.
- *Basement or crawl space:* Is it damp? Is there adequate insulation?
- *Attic:* Is it adequately insulated and vented? Are there any signs of leakage?
- *Quality and workmanship:* Do the cupboard doors hang properly? Do doors open and close well or do they get stuck? Do the door frames and other angles appear to be square? Are the floors firm and level?
- *Apparent energy efficiency:* What type of heating system does the home use? How about air conditioning? How new is it? Is it cost effective? Are the windows single, double, or triple paned? How well is the home insulated?
- *Electrical:* It will be difficult for you to analyze this on your own. But are there any obvious malfunctions such as flickering lights?
- *Plumbing:* How is the water pressure? Turn on the shower and the taps. Is the water quality OK?
- *Appliances:* How old are the major appliances, such as stove, fridge, washer, and dryer? What condition are they in? Will any of them need to be replaced?
- *Exterior:* What shape is the exterior of the home in? Will it need painting or any other type of upkeep soon?
- *Lot:* Does the drainage appear to be OK? That is, does it drain water away from the home? Also, are there any large trees that appear to be too close to the home?
- *Attached or additional structures:* What is the condition of any additions, garages, sheds, workshops, etc.?

CHAPTER 9

Putting It All Together

"I think we've found it!"

Putting It All Together

Where to Find Homes

The first place you'll want to search for a home is through your real estate agent.

After speaking with him or her about your wants and needs, your agent will supply you with a list of homes that meet your criteria.

If you'd like to do some searching before you find an agent, there are lots of places you can look. Start with your local real estate papers or magazines, then go down to local real estate offices and see what they have advertised. You might also want to drive through prospective neighborhoods to see what's available. Talk to friends and coworkers. Maybe they've seen something that would suit you. If you can, attend open houses to get some experience walking through and looking at homes. Try to envision yourself living there. Does this home match your lifestyle?

Another great place to look for homes is on the Internet. Every major real estate company is represented on-line. Just enter their name into a search engine to find their website. They should direct you to properties listed by their offices in your area. Just remember: any properties you do find will be represented by the *seller's* agent.

You can also search for properties on-line by using a Multiple Listing Service (MLS). This is a service that lists and describes every property for sale by real estate brokerages in a given region. Nearly every state or city has an MLS online. Just enter the term "multiple listing service" and the name of your community in a search engine and see what comes up.

Finally, you can also go to www.yahoo.com and enter "real estate." Yahoo is set up so you can browse through real estate sites according to region, state, or country. Other search engines may also be useful.

A word of caution: Don't rely too much on the Internet to help you find a home. The Internet is a great tool, but it has two major drawbacks: One, it doesn't list every home available in your area. Two, much of the information may be out-of-date, depending on how often the site is updated. So be sure to correlate this information with sources in the real world.

How Many Homes Should You Look At?

We recommend that you begin by looking at about twenty homes before making an offer. That may sound like a lot, but the more homes you see, the better feel you will have for what's out there. You're going through a steep learning curve, so better not to rush things. Looking at a number of homes will also make you less likely to get carried away by emotions. The first few homes may impress you, but as you continue your search, you'll develop a much more critical eye. Try to include a number of different home types and styles in your search, even if they don't appeal to you at first. You may be surprised at what you find—and like! A good idea is to set aside a Saturday or some other day of the week and book five or six appointments in a row. That way the homes will be fresh in your mind, making them easier to compare.

Your First Look

The first time you look at a home, you're just trying to get an overall feel for the place on a "gut level." Before you go inside, stop and take a good look at the exterior of the home and the property as a whole. Does it appeal to you? Is it large enough? Small enough? Can you picture yourself suntanning in the backyard? Can you picture someone buying it from you five years down the road?

After you've taken a look at the outside, go inside and do the same thing for the interior. Consult your wish list and reality check periodically, but go more for the feel of the place. Does it feel like home? Can you picture yourself eating breakfast in the kitchen? Don't feel like you have to make a decision as soon as you walk through the door. Relax and enjoy the tour. And try, try, *try* to keep your emotions in check. It's OK to get excited about a home, but be prepared to walk away from all of the homes if they just don't feel right.

Oh, My Aching Head!

When you start home shopping, one of the first things you'll notice is that after looking at a number of properties, the features of each home start to blend together. Did that place on Elm Street have one bathroom or was that the house on Ludwig Avenue? Was that a two-car garage or a carport? And you can't remember.

A simple way to avoid this problem is to keep good notes on every home you visit. This includes noting how each home matches up to your wish list and reality check. Below is a form that will help you keep track of these and other details. Make as many copies of this form as you like, one for each home you visit.

Once you've visited several homes, sit down and compare what you've recorded on these forms with your wish list and reality check to see which seem like the best match. Real estate agents will also provide you with a detailed written description of each home during your tour. This will include such things as square footage, lot size, a description of amenities, a photo of the home, and so forth. This will also help you sort through everything you've seen and remind you of any details you missed.

Take a Second Look

Once you've narrowed down your list of potential homes to three or four, it's time to schedule an appointment for a second walk-through. During this visit, you need to be a lot more rigorous in your examination of the home. How does it measure up to your wish list and reality check? You should also bring along your home inspection checklist from chapter 8 (if you haven't already) and give the home a good going-over. If you have a friend in the construction business, bring that person along. Ask lots of questions, both of the agent and yourself. Be honest: Does this home really suit your needs or have you simply "fallen in love"? Can you see yourself living happily in this location for the next five years? Can you come up with five reasons not to buy the home? Can you then defeat *all* of these objections with sound arguments?

When you finally narrow down your list to a single home, you're ready to start talking turkey. Now turn the page and learn some of the finer points of closing the deal.

Home Shopping Checklist

GENERAL INFORMATION

Property Address: _____

Exterior Description: _____

List Price: $ _____   Property Taxes: $_____ /year

Age: _____

HOME

Condition: _____	Square footage: _____
No. of bedrooms: _____	No. of bathrooms: _____
Living room: _____	Dining room: _____
Kitchen: _____	Family room: _____
Den: _____	Laundry room: _____
Recreation room: _____	Other rooms: _____
Basement: _____	Attic: _____
Heating system: _____	Storage space: _____
Windows: _____	Appliances: _____
Fireplace: _____	Exterior: _____
Roof: _____	Patio or deck: _____
Garage: _____	Other amenities: _____

LOT

Size: _____	Shape: _____
Landscaping: _____	Garden: _____
View: _____	Fence: _____
Slope: _____	Parking: _____

NEIGHBORHOOD

General condition: _____	Traffic: _____
Noise level: _____	Safety/security: _____
Age/type of inhabitants: _____	Parking: _____
Zoning regulations: _____	Snow removal: _____

CONVENIENT TO

Supermarket: _____	Shopping: _____
Schools: _____	Church: _____
Work: _____	Hospital: _____
Parks/recreation: _____	Public transit: _____

CHAPTER 10

Closing the Deal

"So . . . how does it feel?"

"I'm glad it's finally all done. It was scary . . . it was exciting . . . and it took a lot of negotiating, but we pretty much got the deal we wanted."

Closing the Deal

The big day is finally here! You've found your dream home and you're ready to buy it. Now what?

Assessing a Home's Value

When making an offer never, ever pay the asking price. Buyers always leave themselves some room for negotiation. If you're going to buy the home for less, this requires figuring out what the home is worth. There are several ways to do this.

Investigate what other similar homes in the area are selling for. This process is called a comparative market analysis. If you're working with a buyer's agent, he or she will offer this service. If you're not working with a buyer's agent, you can hire a professional home appraiser to do this for you.

Another option is to go on-line. A good place to start is www.homeprice.com. This service maintains a database on 50 million properties in one thousand counties in forty-six states. They create home price indexes.

Consider the condition of the home and property. By now you should have a pretty good idea of what sort of shape the place is in. How does it compare to other homes in the area? Have any major improvements been made to the home? How much do you think these affect the home's value?

Look into market conditions. Fluctuations in supply and demand play a large role in a home's value. A seller's market means there are more buyers than there are homes. In a seller's market, homes often sell within days or weeks of being listed. This heavy demand for housing puts the sellers in the driver's seat when it comes to pricing, allowing them to ask more than they normally would. A buyer's market, on the other hand, means there are more homes than buyers. In this situation, sellers are much more likely to lower their price to make a sale.

Consider the seller's motivation. Real estate agents often talk of "motivated sellers." These are people who are under the gun to get rid of their home. Perhaps there's been some sort of family, financial, or professional crisis that is forcing them to sell. You may be able to shave a few thousand dollars off the price just because they're desperate to get out.

Making an Offer

Now it's time to draw up an official offer. There are two things you should know about this process.

First, all offers must be made in writing and submitted through your real estate agent or lawyer. There is a standard procedure for how to do this, and they will help guide you through it. However, here are the main elements that an offer contains:

- The proposed selling price (your offer).
- Any conditions on your offer. These include concessions you would like the seller to make, as well as situations that may halt the deal, such as if the home fails to pass a home inspection.
- Financing contingencies: for example, your offer may be subject to you being able to get a mortgage.
- A clear definition of what is to be included in the sale. Don't assume that things like swing sets are included. If it isn't nailed down, the seller can take it with him. Make sure you note *everything* you want in your offer.
- The size of your deposit (also called *earnest* money) included with the offer.

The second thing you need to know about making an offer is that doing so is much more serious than it sounds. If you make an offer and the seller accepts, then you have just entered into a *legally binding agreement*. You may not even need to fill out any additional paperwork. Your initial offer now becomes the contract.

But don't panic! Nine times out of ten your first offer will be rejected. Why? Because the seller knows that no one makes his or her best offer the first time around. The first offer is usually a lowball bid. Buyers, like sellers, always leave themselves a bit of "wiggle room" for negotiation. Now he or she will usually return with a counteroffer. This is where your skills as a negotiator come in.

The Art of Negotiation

Good negotiation involves information, preparation, and realism.

Information: You've already gathered most of this in preparation for making your initial offer. This includes your comparative market analysis, researching the condition of the home, the amenities, seller motivation, and so on. When the seller makes a counteroffer, perhaps that is a good time to go back over this information to see if you can find anything to help you come up with a new bid. Perhaps you could concede on some of your terms in lieu of raising your asking price. Or, conversely, perhaps you could agree to increase your asking price if the seller throws in something extra.

Preparation: Buying a home is a highly emotional experience, especially your first time out. You must decide ahead of time that no matter how much you love the home, you will walk away from it if you're not able to purchase it for the price you want and under the conditions you stipulated. Otherwise you run the risk of paying more than the home is worth or agreeing to terms that you will regret later on. If sellers pick up on the fact that you're not willing to walk away, they'll just sit on their price until you finally cough up.

Realism: Don't think you're going to get the home for nothing. Sellers don't pull their asking prices out of a hat. All homes have something called a Fair Market Value (FMV). Therefore, don't insult the seller by offering half of what they're asking. The same goes for offering too much. Don't get so caught up in a bidding frenzy that you lose your head. Walk away, if necessary.

Closing the Deal

Once you're made your offer, negotiations have been completed, the home has been inspected, and your financing is in place, it's time to sign on the dotted line. This finalization or closing process is also called *settlement,* or *escrow*. It involves signing the legal documents, finalizing your mortgage or other financial arrangements, and transferring the title of the home to your name. Once the process is complete, you walk away as the proud owner of a new home!

A Few More Shekels, Please

One thing most first-time homeowners don't count on is the cost of actually closing the deal. First off, you'll have to shell out the remainder of your down payment (whatever is left over after paying your initial deposit). You'll also have to pay any costs related to your mortgage, such as application fees, processing fees, mortgage insurance, and so on. There's also insurance on the new home, which has to be purchased before you buy the home. And then the lawyer steps in. You'll owe fees for drawing up contracts and papers plus disbursement fees for things like title searches and other duties your lawyer carries out on your behalf. Believe it or not, all of these closing fees combined can add a few thousand dollars to the price of your home.

Your lender will discuss these costs with you when you negotiate your mortgage. Many lenders will also allow you to roll these costs into your loan so you don't have to pay them out of your own pocket. However, if you can pay them up front, that will be better. Otherwise you'll wind up paying interest on these costs as part of your mortgage.

Conclusion

You can see why we said at the beginning that buying a home is one of the most significant and complicated decisions you will ever make. However, now that you're armed with information, you're a lot closer to buying your dream home than when you started. Just trust God, keep your feet on the ground, and you can't go wrong! Happy hunting!

Glossary

Adjustable rate mortgage: A mortgage with an interest rate that fluctuates according to a mortgage index, causing your monthly mortgage payment to increase or decrease accordingly.

Amortization period: The period of time over which your mortgage payments are spread out. The longer the amortization period, the lower your payments, and vice versa.

Buyer's agent: A real estate agent that represents the buyer, not the seller.

Debt service ratio: The ratio of your total debt versus your total income.

Deed: The document that states who owns a particular piece of property.

Down payment: The amount of money you put down on a home up front, usually between 5 and 20 percent of the home's value.

Earnest money: A deposit submitted with your offer to show that you're serious about buying the home.

Escrow: Funds held in reserve prior to closing to pay for taxes, homeowners insurance, and other closing costs.

Fixed rate mortgage: A mortgage with a fixed interest rate that does not change during the lifetime of the loan.

Mortgage: A loan that you take out in order to buy a home.

Mortgage broker: A company that processes home loan applications and then shops around among various lenders to find the best mortgage for a client.

Mortgage insurance: Insurance that borrowers purchase to protect the lender in case the borrower defaults on the loan.

Preapproved mortgage: A mortgage option that allows you to have your loan approved before you go shopping for a home.

Principal: The actual amount of money you borrow from a lender. The lender charges interest as a percentage of the principal.

Real estate broker: A real estate agent who belongs to the National Association of Realtors. Only real estate brokers are allowed to open a real estate agency.

Seller's agent: A real estate agent that represents the seller, not the buyer.

Index

Larry Burkett's Stewardship for the Family™ provides the practical tips and tools that children and parents need to understand biblical principles of stewardship. Its goal is *"Teaching Kids to Manage God's Gifts—Time, Talents and Treasures."* Stewardship for the Family™ materials are adapted from the works of best-selling author on business and personal finances, **Larry Burkett**. Larry is the author of more than 60 books and hosts the radio programs *Money Matters* and *How to Manage Your Money,* aired on more than 1,100 outlets worldwide. Visit Larry's website at www.mm4kids.org